THIS BOOK

BELONGS TO:

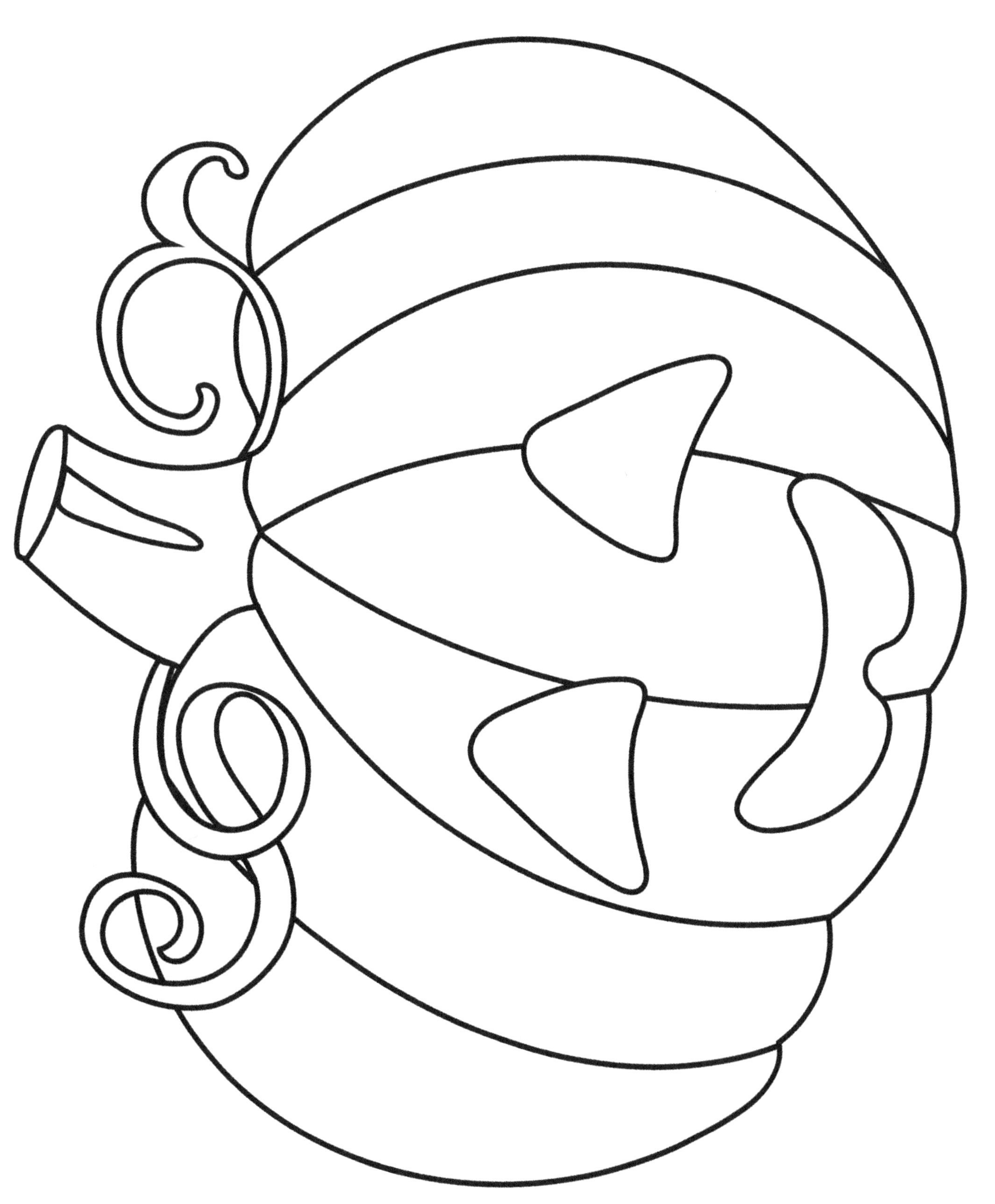

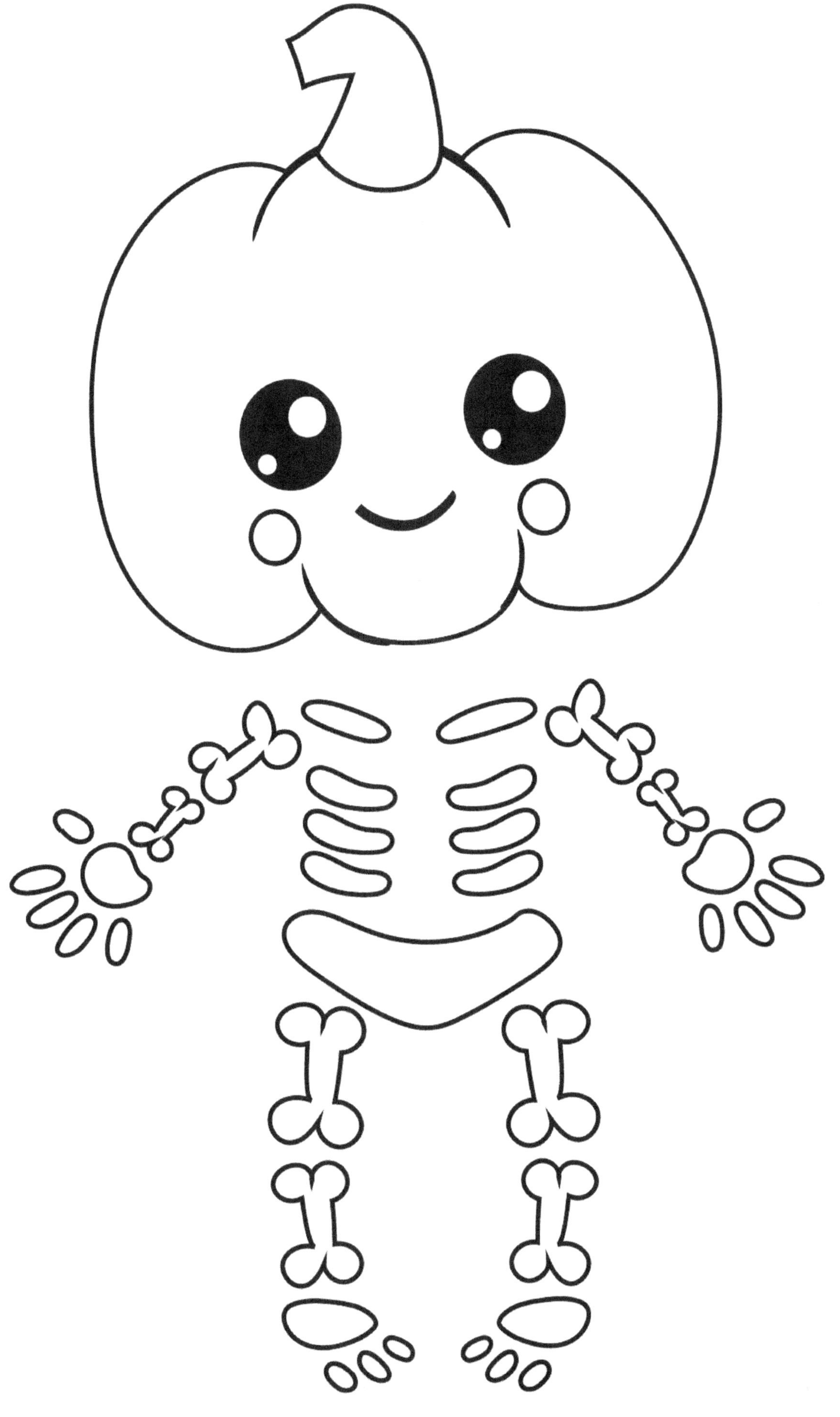

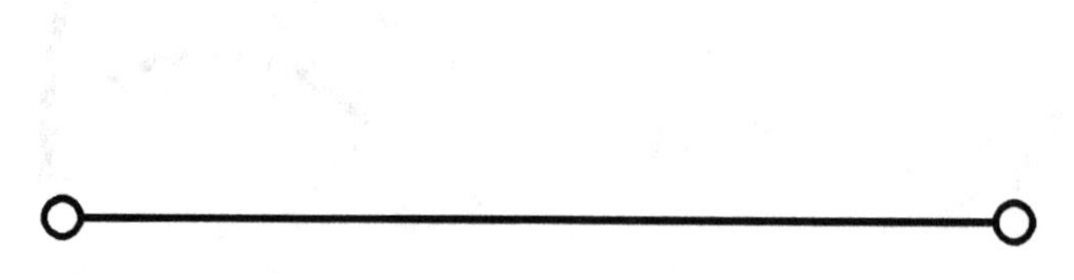

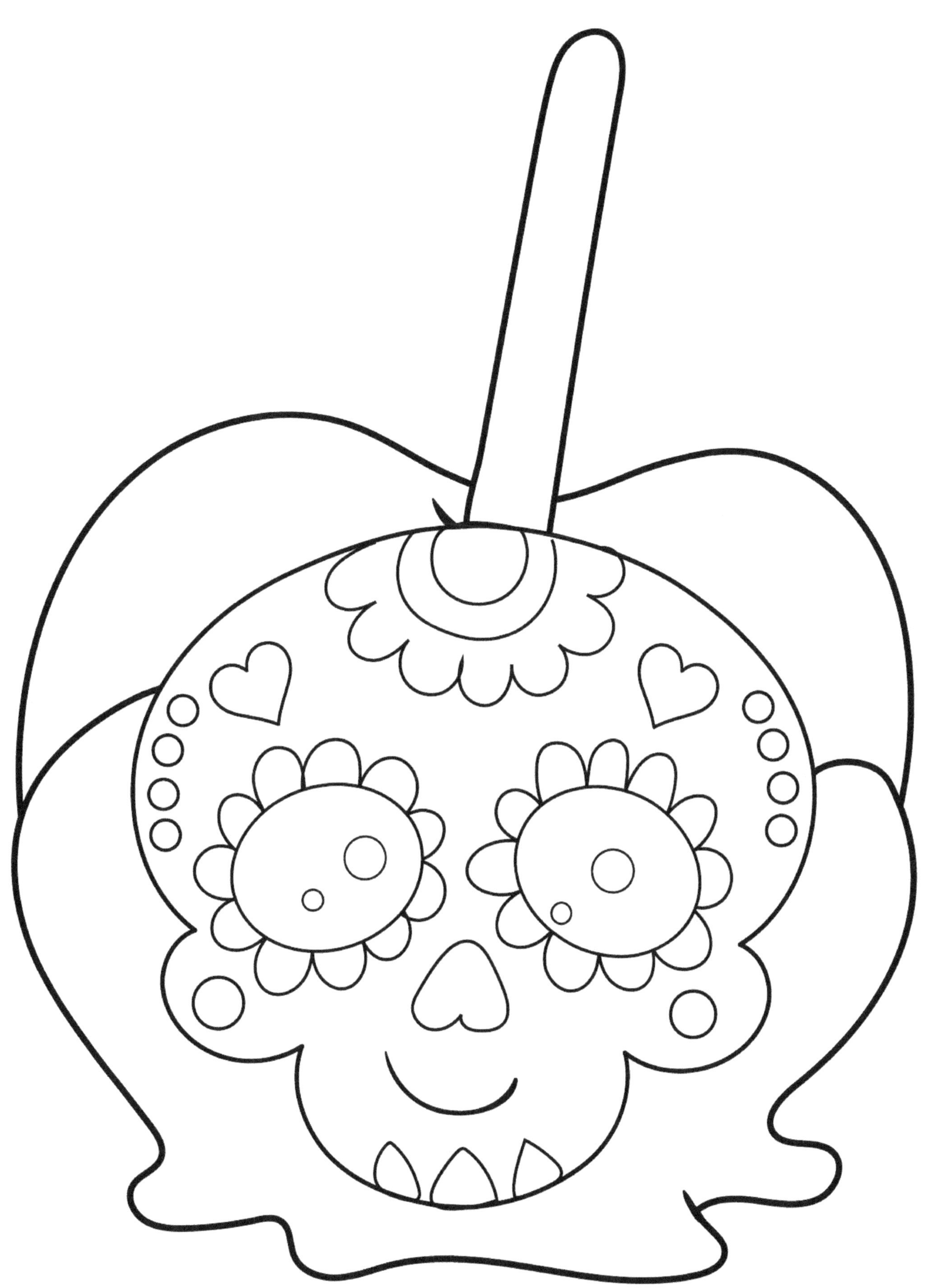

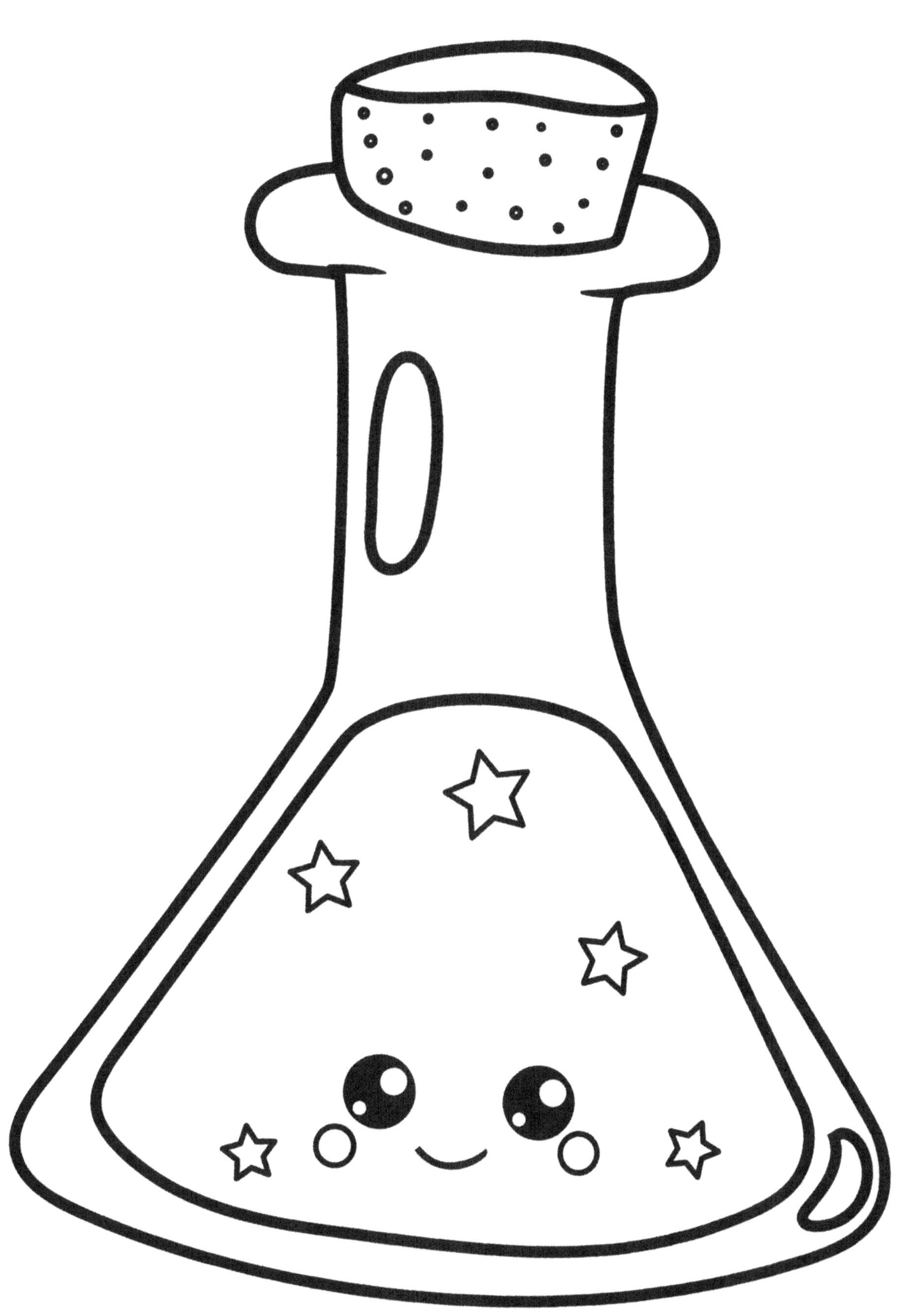

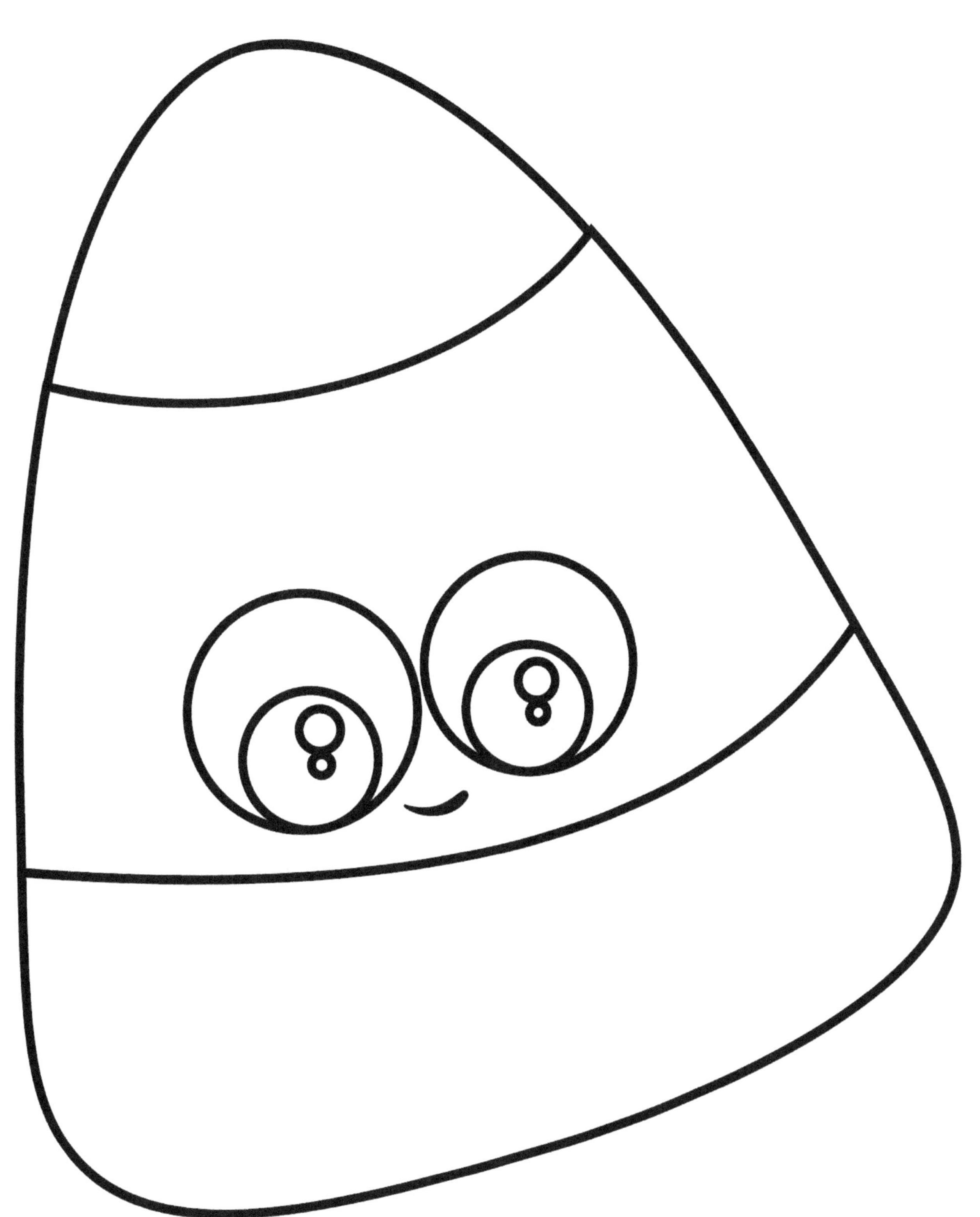

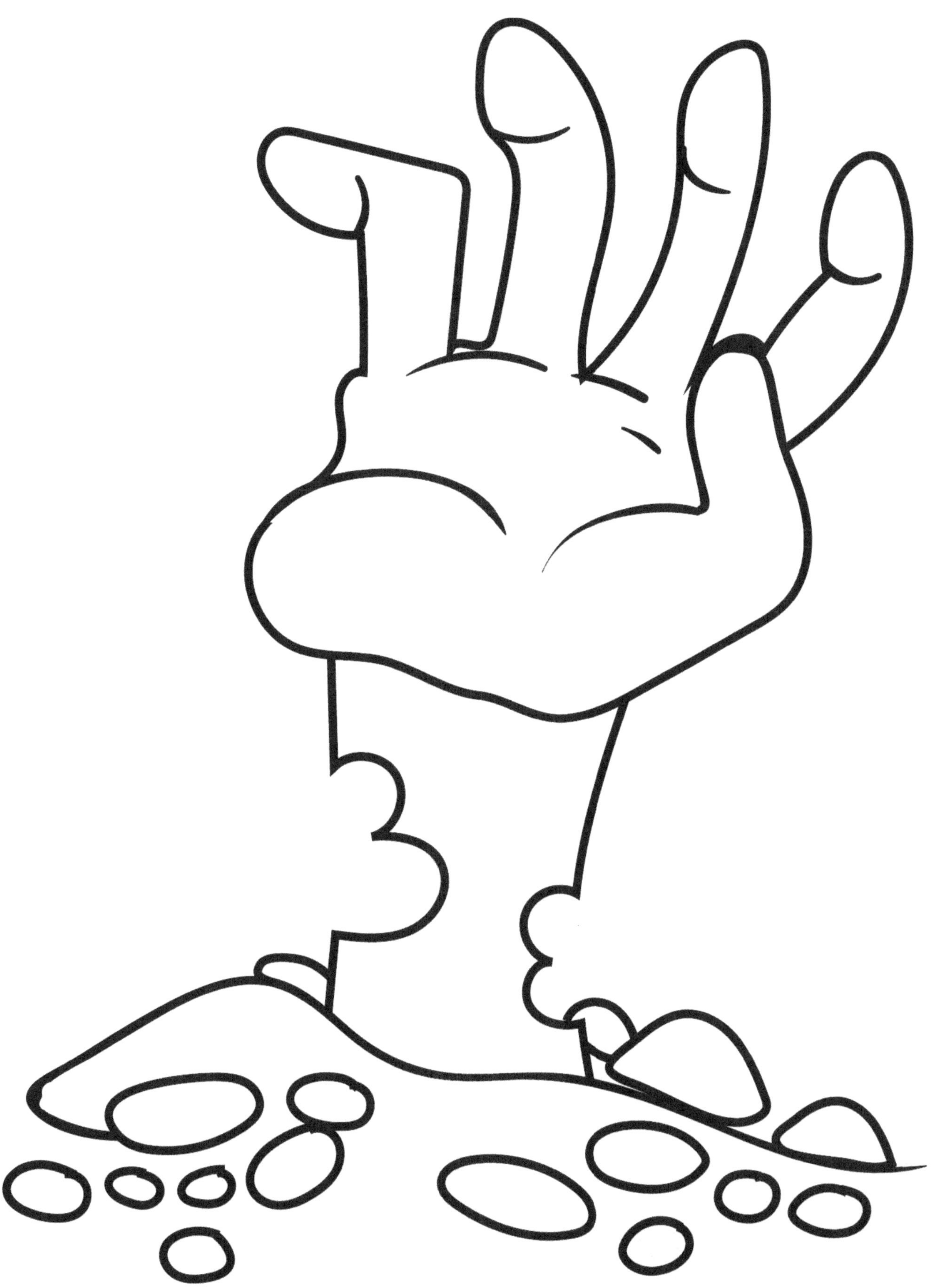

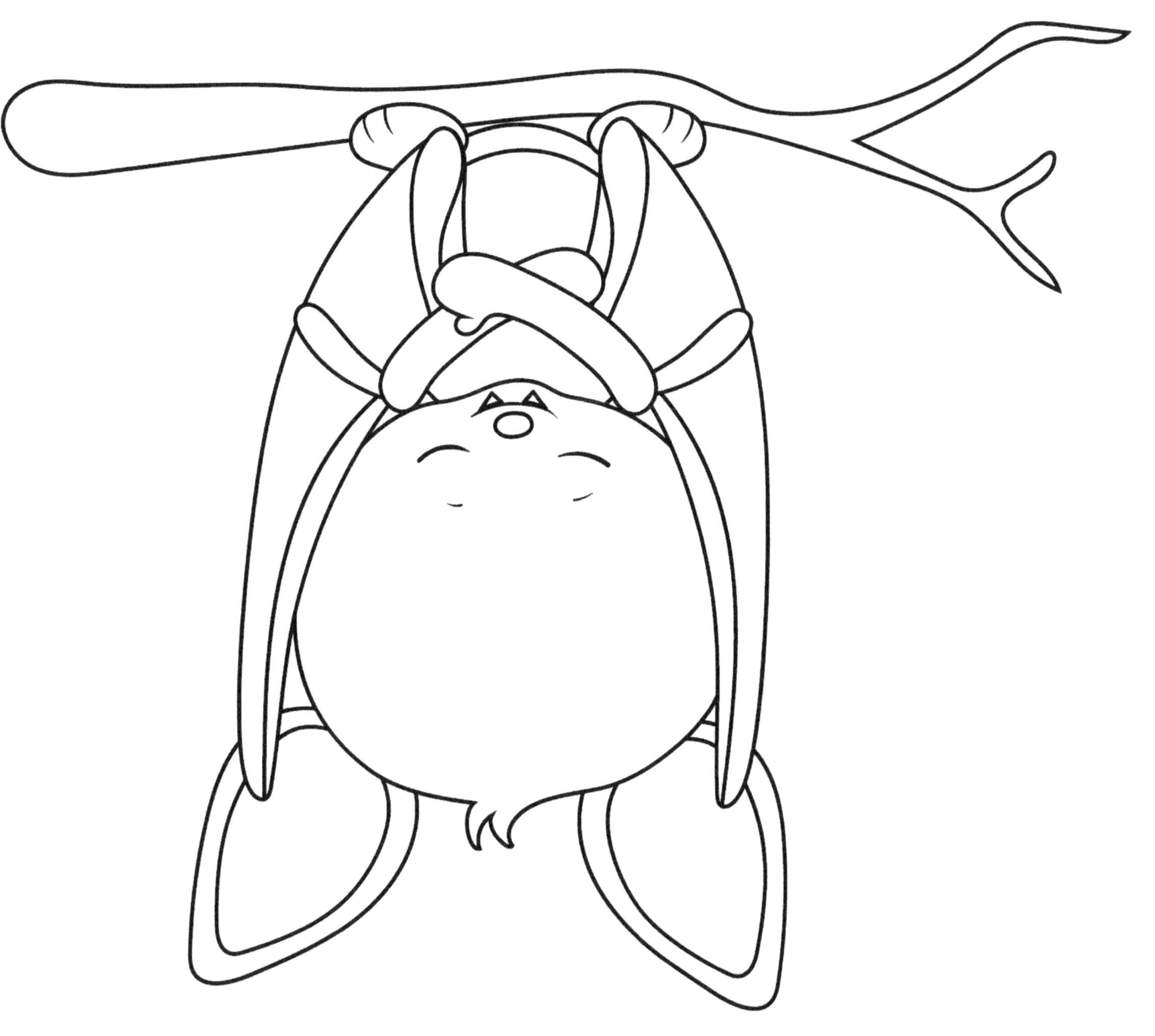

BOO

RIP

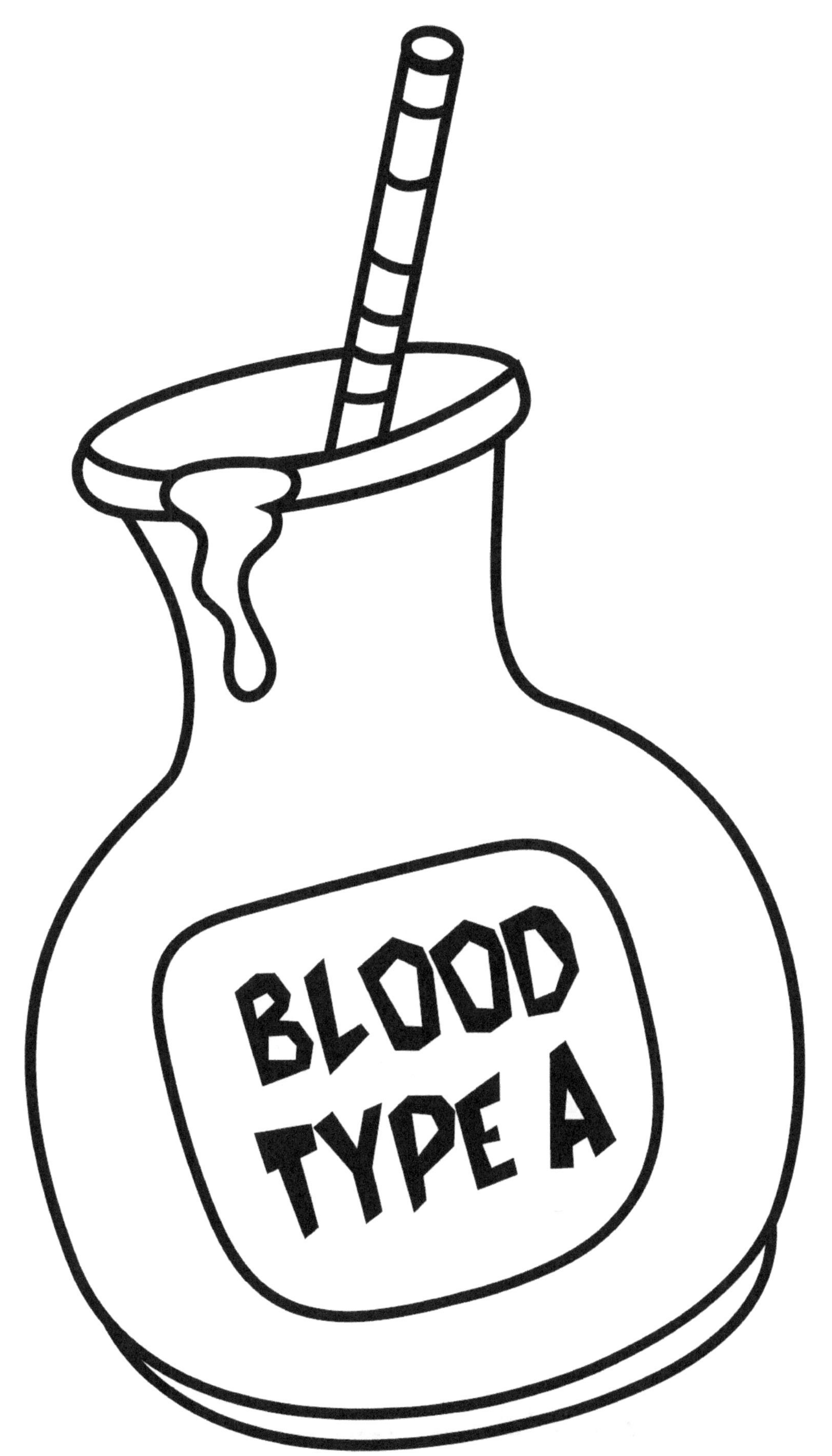
BLOOD
TYPE A

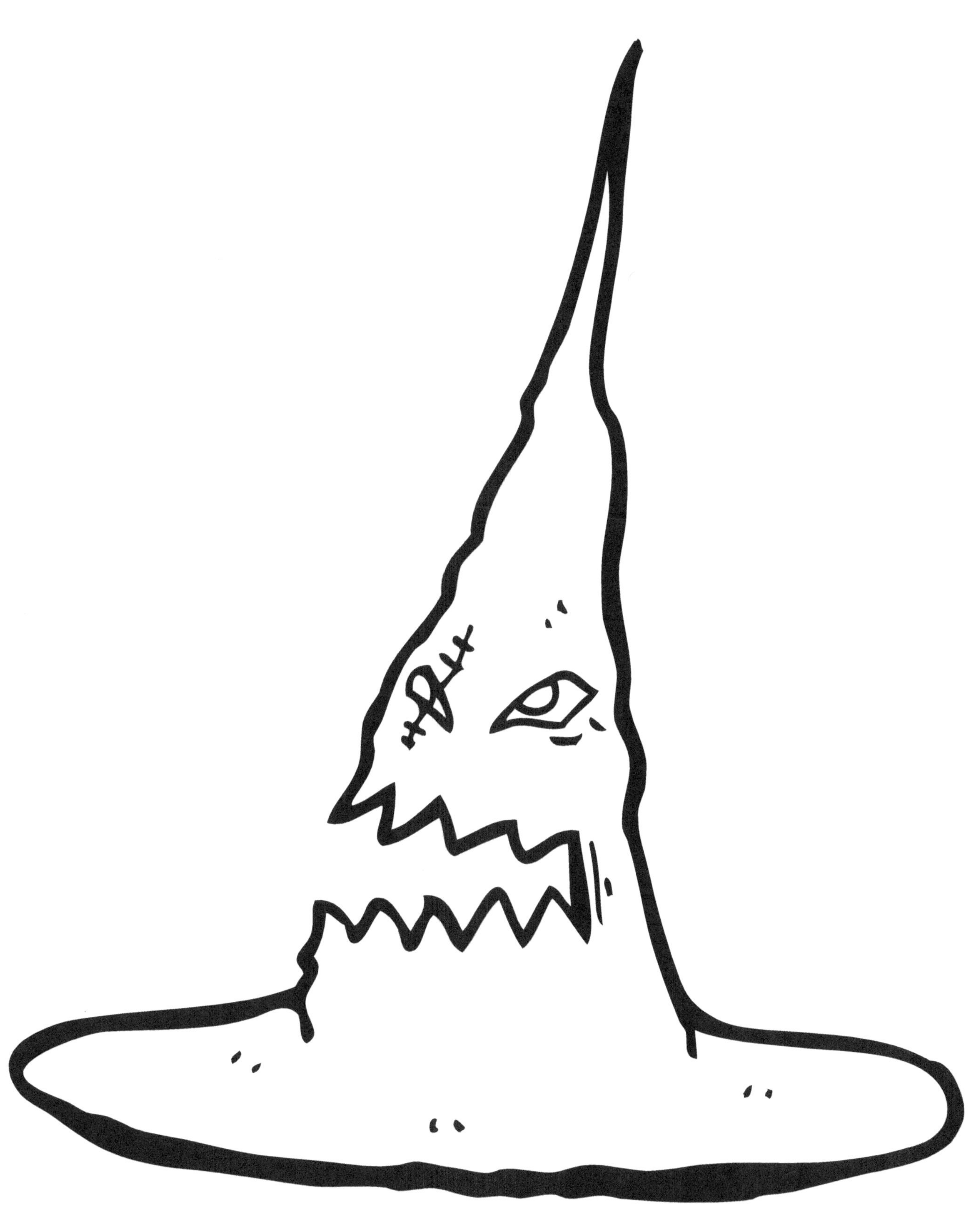